Climb

How to plan, prepare and Su ... ...climb the world's tallest free standing mountain.

Aristarick Benard and Wayne Evans

ISBN-13: 978-1539927952

ISBN-10: 1539927954

For our 4 amazing children… shine your bright light wherever you go.

Why You Should Read This?

If you plan to climb Kilimanjaro, then this useful guide provides tips, strategies and the routes to the peak.

'Climbing Kilimanjaro' is written by lead guide whom has peaked 80 times. The information passed to you is based on qualifications and experience.

Table of Contents:

Chapter 1 – The Tourists Cities

Arusha

Despite being tagged as Tanzania's 'Safari's Capital', it is often overlooked (unfairly, in my opinion) in favour of it's better known and more glamorous neighbours, Serengeti, Lake Manyara and Ngorongoro Conservation area.

However, Arusha offers Tourists a wealth of cultural experiences, ranging from safaris in the National Park to taking hikes on Mount Meru and a tour for Tanzanite and much more.

Arusha town has a population of 3.5 million. It origins began as a German settlement on the Boma Road built by Maasai labour. The planting of sisal tea and coffee thrived and the city flourished and became known as the Geneva of Africa. It is also home to the International Human Rights Tribunal.

Kilimanjaro's airport of Bouder is also located nearby and serves both local and international flyers, making gems like the Island of Zanzibar and remote safari camps just a plane ride away.

Agriculture and tourism are the two main pillars of Arusha's economy. You can tour of the coffee plantation, take Tanzania cookery courses, and attend workshops in drum making and batik providing an insight into local life.

Home to the famous Maasai Warriors with their red 'Shukas', decorated (beaded jewellery) spears and their nomadic warrior traditions. You can attend guided tours whereby they open up their village for inspection for anything from half a day to three days. During this time, you can walk through the forest gathering plants with a traditional healer, make cheese and Ugali (dish of flour cooked with water to a dough like consistency) with the women, learn their traditional songs and soak up their pastoral lifestyle.

If you enjoy souvenir shopping, Arusha is a noted craft centre. The cultural heritage centre in the town boast an array of superb the Makonde (Tribe) carvings, gorgeous tingatinga paintings, gifts and curios. If you want more exclusive gifts, Arusha is about the best place to buy Tanzanite (a brilliant blue gemstone found in the hills surrounding Arusha and Moshi). The gem stone is used by the Maasai to celebrate birth and gained international prominence after Tanzanite was featured in the movie 'Titanic' as the centre jewel in the 'Heart of the Ocean' necklace.

Finally, at night, a relaxed atmosphere descends on Arusha with Jazz, Salsa and local hip hop 'traditional' music and full moon parties in the bush. Dinner is covered through a variety of restaurants, offering Swahili, Indian and international cuisine. So if been on Safari or Mountain climbing, Arusha is definitely well worth a visit.
Chapter 23--

Dar es Saalam

Dar es Saalam translates as the 'harbour of peace'. The name was bestowed on the city during the time of Sultan Seyyid Majid, whom chose the sleeping fishing village of Zaramo to have his summer palace, Bandur. The village thrived on ivory and slaves, transforming over time into a bustling city, which became known as Dar es Salaam.

The city is a hotchpotch of cultural and religious influences. The Arabs, Indians, Germans and British have all contributed to Architecture, whilst Seiks, Muslims, Hindus and Christian co-exist peacefully with the willing of the Azan blending into the sound of church bells in the morning.

In the city of Kariakoo, in the bustling market, Chinese electronics sit side by side with Chickens, cheerful tingating paintings are stacked next to folded piles of 'Khangas' (African wraps) and 'Kitenge' (similar to sarongs). Traditional medicines share floor space with pyramids of fruit and vegetables as shopkeepers wait for opportunities.

Visitors to Dar es Salaam are catered for through a variety of accommodation and for all budgets too, whether that's backpackers in simple hostels, through to five star hotels for the business traveller. Restaurants offer Indian, Italian, Japanese, Ethiopian and more as well as local restaurants serving Chips, Ugali, and Nyama Choma (grilled goat/sheep meat) and fresh grilled other meat.

Dar es Salaam has an electric live music scene .Traditional 'Taarabu' (popular music genre) orchestras rub shoulders with dance bands playing Jazz, Salsa and Afro funk, Rap and African hip hop (known as Bongo Flava). Dar es Saalam also hosts the annual Euro Africa film festival too.

'Nyumba ya Sanaa' (Nyerere cultural centre) exhibits art and hand crafts throughout the year and allows visitors to take part in painting workshops and etching. The National Museum and Botanical Gardens are a great way to spend a day tracing the history of Tanzania.

Moshi Town

Moshi town lies just minutes from Kilimanjaro airport and is only town that lies close to all routes up Kilimanjaro. With a population of just 900,000 predominantly made up by the 'Chagga' tribe.

Visitors still have a good choice of accommodation, ranging from budget for back packers through to three star hotels. Restaurants offerings range from Indian, Italian and Chinese through to the traditional noted in Dar es Saalam. There's music in the evening too with everything from jazz to local hip hop!

Agriculture and Tourism are the two main pillars of Moshi's economic success. Tours of the coffee plantation are good as well as Tanzania cookery courses. I recommend going to Lake Chala too.

Chapter Two: Tanzania

Tanzania is a land of utter contrast. From the snow capped peak of Mount Kilimanjaro to endless plains of the Serengeti and the sun kissed islands of Zanzibar. It was here, in the Olduvai Gorge, that early man left his first footprints and it was here on Parlm in Zanzibar, that Swahili traders welcomed trading boats from across the Indian ocean

Geography
Tanzania lies between latitudes 1°00 and 11° 00s and longitudes 30°00 and 40°00E. Three hours ahead of Greenwich Mean Time (GMT + 3 hours). The area of Tanzania is 939,701 sq km including the islands of Zanzibar, Pema and Mafia and 53,000sq km is inland water.

The physical features of Tanzania are the coastal plains, plateaus, valleys, rivers, Miombo woodland and Mountains.

Climate
Tanzania's climate is generally tropical but temperate in the highlands. The Central Plateau is dry and arid with hot days and cool nights, but June to September is the cool season. The wet season is from March to May and the dry period ranges from October and February.

On the coast, it rains in November and December and from March to May. Coastal areas are hot and humid although sea breezes cool the area pleasantly between June and September.

Clothing.
For holiday travellers doing Safaris in the North, light clothing, sturdy shoes and canvas hats during the day are recommended. At night, casual clothes with a light cardigan or pullover (for altitudes between 1,500 metres in Arusha and 2,400 metres in Ngorongoro). On the coast, summer wear!

Trekker bound for Kilimanjaro or other treks, should check with a mountain specialist before departure. Bring sunscreen, after sun, sunglasses, mosquito cream and binoculars.

On Safari avoid brightly coloured clothes as this may alarm the animals. Browns, beiges and Khaki are preferred as are short sleeved shirts/ blouses and shorts. It can be chilly in the early morning and in evening, so pack a jumper too. Finally, don't forget a swimsuit. However, 'bareing' too much will offend to local traditions

The History

Northern Tanganyika's famed Olduvai Gorge has provided rich evidence of the areas prehistoric past, including fossil remains of some of humanity's earliest ancestors. Discoveries suggest that east Africa may have been the site of human origin.

Little is known of the history of Tanganyika's interior during the early centuries of the Christian occupation. Tribes were gradually displaced by Bantu farmers migrating from the West and South and by Nilotes and related northern people. Some of these groups had well organized societies and controlled extensive areas by the time the Arab slavers, European explorers and missionaries penetrated the interior in the first half of the 19th century.

The coastal area welcomed visitors as early as the 8th Century as traders arrived and in the 12th century, traders and immigrants came from as for away as Persia (now Iran) and India.

They built a series of highly developed cities and trading sites along the coast with the principal one being Kibaha (a settlement of Persian origin) that held as cadency until the Portuguese destroyed it in the early 1500's.

The Portuguese navigator, Vasco da Gama explored the East African coast in 1498 on his voyage to India. By 1506, the Portuguese claimed control over the entre coast. This control was weak though because they did not colonize the area or explore the interior.

Assisted by Omani Arabs, the indigenous coastal dwellers succeeded in driving the Portuguese from the area North of the Ruvuma River by the early 18th Centaury. Omani Sultan Sayyid Said (1804 – 56) moved his capital to Zanzibar in 1841.

European exploration of the interior began in the mid 19th century as two German missionaries reached Mount Kilimanjaro in the 1840's. British explorers Richard Buston and John Speke also crossed the interior to Kike Tanganyikain 1857. David Livingstone, the Scottish missionary and explorer who crusaded against the slave trade, established his last mission at Ujiji, where he was found by Henry Morton Stanley, the American journalist/explorer whom had been commissioned by the New York Herald to locate him.

German colonial interests were initiated in 1884 by Kar Peters, whom formed 'The Society for German Colonization', after he concluded a series of treaties with Tribal Chief's who accepted German protection. Prince

Otto von Bismarck's government established the German East African Company.

In 1886 and 1890, Anglo – German agreements were negotiated that agreed control in the interior of East Africa and along the coastal strip previously claimed by the Omani Sultan of Zanzibar.

In 1891, the German Government took over direct administration of the territory from the German East Africa Company and appointed a Governor with headquarters at Dar es Salaam.

Although the German colonial administration brought cash, crops, railroads and roads to Tanganyika, European rule provoked Africans resistance, culminating in the Majimaji rebellion of 1905 – 07. The rebellion (which temporarily united a number of southern tribes) only ended after an estimated 120, 000 Africans deaths from fighting or starvation. This was the first sings of Nationalism.

German colonial domination of Tanganyika ended after World War I when control of most of the territory passed to the United Kingdom under a league of Nations mandate. After World War 2, Tanganyika became a UN territory under British control. Subsequent years witnessed Tanganyika progressing to self government and independence.

In 1954, Julius K. Nyerere, a school teacher whom was then one of only two Tanganyikan's educated abroad at the University level, organized a political party, namely, Tanganyika African National Union (TANU). TANU supported candidates whom were victorious in the legislative council elections of September 1958 and February 1959. In December of that year, the United Kingdom agreed to the establishment of internal self – governance following general elections to be held in August 1960, which succeeded.

In May 1961 Tanganyika became autonomous and Nyerere became Prime Minister under a new constitution. Full independence was achieved on December 9, 1961. Mr Nyerere was elected President when Tanganyika became a Republic within the Commonwealth a year after independence.

Zanzibar
Zanzibar's political development began in earnest after 1956 when provision was first made for the election of six non Government members to the legislative council. Two parties were formed, namely the Zanzibar Nationalist Party (ZNP) representing the dominant Arab

and 'Arabised' minority and the Afri–Shirazi Party (ASP) whom represented the Shirazi's and the African majority.

The first elections were held in July 1957 the ASP won three of the six elected seats, with the remainder going to independents. Later, the ASP split, with some of its Shirazi Supporters forming the Zanzibar and Pemba People's Part (ZPPP).

On April 26 1964, Tanganyika united with Zanzibar to form the United Republic of Tanganyika and Zanzibar. This was renamed the United Republic of Tanzania on October 29th 1964.

United Republic of Tanzania

To form one ruling party, Nyerere merged TANU with the Zanzibar ruling party, the ASP of Zanzibar to form CCM (Chama cha Mapinduzi - Revolutionary party) on February 5 1977. The CCM was to be the sole instrument for mobilizing and controlling the population in all significant political or economic activities.

He envisioned the party as a 'two way street' for the flow of ideas and policy directives between village level and the Government. On April 26, 1977 the union of the two parties was ratified in a new Constitution. The merger was reinforced by later Constitutions.

Nyerere stepped down from Office and was succeeded as President by Ali Hassan Mwinyi in 1985. Nyerere retained his position as Chairman of the ruling party for 5 more years and was influential in Tanzania politics until his death in October 1999.

Current President is Dk. Shane, whom was elected in 2010.

The people and language.

The Republic of Tanzania is one of Africa's most peaceful countries. Home to a flourishing Democracy and prosperous economy, the country is known for its peace and security.

With a population of 45 million, the Tanzanian people are a diverse mix of traditional tribes, village farmers and cosmopolitan professionals. United by a common language, Swahili and a strong sense of national community. Tanzania has more than 120 tribes and are free to worship what ever religion they like. Swahili is the national language East Africa in general.

The Economy

Agriculture is the mainstay of Tanzania's Economy, employing about 80% of the work force and accounting for close to 50% of gross domestic product (GDP). Major commercial crops include Coffee, Tea, Cotton, Cashews and Sisal.

Tourism

Tourism is playing an increasingly important role in the economy and is now the country largest earner of foreign currency. According to figures from Tanzania Tourism Directorate, more than 600,000 visitors came to Tanzania in 1999 – 2000, bringing in revenue of over US $7,000 million. This is up from about 200,000 visitors and US $120 million in the early 1990's.

Mining

Accounts for only circa 1.5% of (GDP), but nevertheless is an important sector. Revenues have increased in recent years due to an expansion of gold and diamond exports. Several new gold mining projects have been initiated in the Lake Victoria region and Tanzania is predicted to be Africa's third largest gold producer behind South Africa and Ghana.

Tanzania currency

Tanzania shillings prevail, however you are advised to carry American Dollar. Bureau de Change's do accept major convertible currencies including the EURO and the Japanese Yen. Travellers Cheques may be acceptable in some places, but not in the remote countryside. Major Credit Cards may also be acceptable in some large hotels, however. It is advisable to carry cash (US Dollars), which you will change on arrival.

Tanzania Visa's.

Visas are required to enter Tanzania. They can either be obtained in advance through the various Embassies or High Commissions/Consulates at home, or at the airports or other entry points. The process is swift and easy; all one requires to have, is a valid Passport.

Airport and arrival information.

Three international airports support the country. Dar es Salaam, now know as Julius Nyerere International Airport (JKIA), Kilimanjaro International Airport (KIA) and Zanzibar International Airport.

For Safaris in Northern Tanzania, most visitors are advised to book with an airline whose arrivals and departures are at Kilimanjaro International Airport (KIA), which is 45 minutes drive from Arusha town. Examples are Air Tanzania, KLM Royal Dutch, Gulf Air, Kenya Airways, Ethiopia Airlines and Emirates. It is also possible to get flights transfers from Nairobi (Kenya) too.

Immunization/ vaccination

Vaccination requirements change from time to time, so we suggest you consult your Doctor or health clinic for up to date information on the latest health precautions.

Currently, shots against yellow fever and cholera are recommended but not mandatory. As a precaution, we usually advise anti malaria drugs to be taken before, during and after your visit to Tanzania.

Also, if you are on prescription medication, please ensure that you have an adequate supply to last the duration of your stay and a copy of your prescription.

Geology

Mount Kilimanjaro has three volcanic cones; Kibo, Mawenzi and Shira and is a dormant volcanic mountain.

The structural geology of Mount Kilimanjaro is an interesting one. This is ordinary mountain by the way, but an enormous 'Start' volcano. 'Start' volcanoes are formed when erupted ash and cinders mix with lava flows, then cool to produce a steep conical formation. These types usually take tens of thousands of years to fully materialize and could consist of number of lava forms.

On the Marangu route, you will come across a number of small cone shaped hills. These are known as 'parasitic' cones and are quite simply the off shoots of the main lava flow. In the event that you do the optional saddle walk, you will pass a cliff face that appears to be stained with black and white stripes, known as Zebra Rock. This is the result of mineral rich rain water flowing down from the rocks above and streaking the almost black lava cliff white.

The formations on Kilimanjaro are not limited to volcanic rocks alone, but also include incredibly impressive glacial configurations. Thousands of years ago, huge sheets of ice covered the mountain all the way down to almost 2500m. Today, they can only be seen near the peak and Scientist's predict sadly that within the next 6 years, the snow cap may just disappear completely, confining the sight of the great white peaked mountain to the pages of literature and the memories of those lucky enough to see it in its glory.

History the origin of the name

The origin of the name Kilimanjaro is not precisely known, but a number of theories exist. European explorers had already adopted the name by 1860 and reported that 'Kilimanjaro' was the mountain's Swahili name, but according to the 1987 edition of the Nutgall Encyclopaedia, the name of the mountain was Kilima - njaro.

Johann Ludwig Krapf wrote in 1860 that Swahili along the coast called the mountain 'Kilimanjaro' and claimed that 'Kilimanjaro' meant either mountain of greatness or mountain of caravans. Under the latter meaning 'Kilima' meant 'maintain' and 'njaro' possibly meant 'caravans'.

Generally though, the term Kilima – Njaro is understood to mean the Mountain (Kilima) of greatness (Njaro), although I believe that this could mean 'white' mountain, i.e. denoting whiteness and this is supported by findings with interior tribes.

What is interesting locally, is that the mountain is not known under one name, but the two masses which are part of it, namely Kibo and Kimawenzi.

The Germans on the Kili
In the 1880s the mountain became part of German East Africa and was called 'Kilima – Ndscharo'.

On 6 October 1889 Hans Meyer reached the highest summit on the Crate ridge on Kibo. He named it 'Kai–ser–Wilhelm-Spitze' (after Kaiser Wilhelm Spitze). That name was apparently used until Tanzania was formed in 1964, when the summit was renamed Uhuru meaning 'freedom peak' in Swahili .

The Kaiser Wilhelm Spitze with an altitude of 5,895m (19,340ft) was known at that time to be the highest mountain in the German Empire.

Climbing history
According to the famous English geographer Helford Mackinder, it was the missionary Rebmann of Mombasa who in 1948, first reported the existence of Kilimanjaro in 1861. German officer Baron Carl Claus von der Dacken and a young British geologist, Richard Thornton (1838 – 1863) made the first recorded attempt to climb Kibo, but quite at 8,200 feet/ 2500m. In 1862, von der Decken tried a second time together with Atto Karsten. They reached a height of 14,000 feet (4,280m).

In 1887, Hans Meyer tried and gave up at the base of Kibo. The following year, Meyer planned another attempt with cartographer Oscar Banmann, but the mission was aborted due to the Abushir Revolt.

In 1889, Meyer returned to Kilimanjaro with the celebrated Austrian mountaineer Ludwig Purtscheller for his third attempt. Their climbing team included a local guide Mzee Yohani Kinyala Launco and this time succeeded.

The summit of Kibo wouldn't be climbed again for another 20 years when the Surveyor M. Langein returned in 1909.

In 1989, a committee formed to celebrate the 100th year of the first ascent, decides to award Posthumous Certificates to the African guides and porters who had accompanied Meyer and Purtscheller. Yohani Kinyula Lauwo attended too who had climbed Kili 3 times before the First World War

Climate

There are two seasons, November to December and March to May, with the driest months Between August to October. Rainfall decreases rapidly with increase in altitude, so you will get 2,300 millimetres (mm) in the forest belt (at 1,830m)down to less than 200mm at Kibo hut (4,630m), giving desert like conditions. The prevailing winds are from the Southeast, meaning North facing slopes receive for less rainfall.

January to March are the warmest months. Conditions above 4,000m can be extreme and the temperatures range tremendously. Mist frequently envelopes much of the massif but denser cloud cover is now rare.

Speckles Mousebird

Colobus

Lammergeyer

Blue Monkey

Chapter 4 - The Flora and Fauna of Kilimanjaro

The land covering Kilimanjaro comprises of five ecological zones. Plants there are either unique to that zone or may be found in another. As you climb Kilimanjaro, you meet the following:

The Cultivated Zone
This is an area beginning at 800m climbing to 1800m. In this zone, most of the plants are either food crops or cash crops like Maize, Potatoes, Banana, Beans, Sogham, Millet (grasses), Carrots and Coffee.

The Forest Zone
The forest begins at 1800m and ascends to 2800m. The forest receives the most rain on the mountain, which supports many flora and fauna. The most common plants of the forest are Inpartion Kilimanjari, Pseudoviola, Fireball Lily, Drancaena Afromontna, Thunbergia Alata, Yellow Stink Wood, White Dombey and Repandum.

Healthy Moorland
The Moorland covers the altitude between 2800m to 4000m. The higher you go, the fewer the plants and apart from Sinecio Kilimanjari, no other tall plant inhibits this zone, just grass and shrubs. The common plants found here are giant Lobelia, St Johns Warts, Euryops Dacydiolidiesk Thomsonii (red hot poker), Sinecio Kilimanjari, Artemisia Afra Disa Sairsii and Crdus Deknee. Flora here are, Gladitus watsonides, prorea kilimanjari, beardidlichens transfolium usambariensis and helichrysum meyeri johannis.

The Alpine Desert Zone
This sits between 4000m to 5000m. This is an Alpine Desert where plants have to survive in drought conditions. Rainfall here is less than 180mm per year and coupled with the colder climate but intense sun around the saddle, only three species of tussock grass exist and at approx 4700m you will also find 'Asteraceae', a bright yellow daisy like flower.

The Summit Zone
The final stretch of the mountain (the summit zone) is inhabited only by lichens due to the fact that all water at this altitude has been sucked into the absorbent volcanic rock. At this altitude, even the lichens grow incredibly slowly.

The Fauna

When you think about Kilimanjaro, you must give its Fauna a thought too. It is so abundant.

The forest is home to several different animals like Buffalo on the Alpine desert looking for minerals. The northern side is very close to Amboseli National park in Kenya, so migrating animals move across the border from ambosel The Western side on the other hand touches Arusha National Park (ANP), so animals rotate for one side of ANP, to the west side of Kilimanjaro.

The common animals of Kilimanjaro are black and white Columbus Monkey, Olive Baboon, Civet, Mongoose, Servant, Bush Pig, Honey Badger, Porcupine, Bush Babies, Tree Hyrax, Small Sported Genet, Leopard, Fourstrubs Mouse, Climbing Mouse, Eland, Elephant, Buffalo and Zebra.

Kilimanjaro is also home to a huge species of birds. 280 no less! The forest provides shelter and the common birds of prey are the Auger Buzzard and Lammergeyer, commonly known as Bonmarro.

Other common birds that live on Kilimanjaro are: Silvery Cheeked Hornbills, White Necked Raven, Tropical Boubou, Stonechat, Common Bulbul, Ruppells Robin Chat Speckled Mousebird, Alpine Chart, Streaky Seed Eater, Scarlet tufted Malachite sunbird, Lammergeyer, Crowne Eagle, White Eyed Kikuyu, Hartlaub Turaco Sunbird and Wiver.

Erica Eccelsa

Red Hot Poker

Carduus Keniensis

Wild Protea

Gladiolus

Helichrysum Kilimanjaro (Yellow)

Helichrysum Meyeri Johannis

Impatiens Pseudoviola

Gladiolus

Hartlaubs Turaco

Streaky Seed-Eater

Chapter 5 - Preparation

What ever your inspiration is for wanting to climb Kilimanjaro (or any other mountain for that matter) is admirable? The realty however, is that hiking a mountain is a big challenge. Whilst hiking will keep you fit, climbing a mountain presents unfamiliar circumstances so you learn to deal with them.

This book highlights the positives of visiting Tanzania and indeed Kilimanjaro but the question you might be asking.... how do I go about going, where do I stay? What gear to take? Which company could organise my tour and guides?

Many of the questions can be answered by Google'ing' Tanzania. Take time to consider the each web site looking for positive vibes about their site. Better still ask friends who have already been and get them to recommend their travel company or Kilimanjaro guides.

Once you have decided on your travel company, use their address to apply for your Visa but keep in your mind that Tanzania is very open for tourism. You could do it on-line or visit Tanzania Embassy on your country.

Training for Kili is very important. Remember, it is the highest point in Africa, so you should walk/train maybe twice to four times a week for three or four hours with seven kg on your back. Remember to wear the boots that you're going to use on Kili, this will prevent you from getting blisters whilst climbing it

Consultant your Doctor before you go. They will advise you on your Country's advice for inoculations. They will also assist you with tablets for high altitude sickness and what medicine's to take.

The company you hire will provide you with a 'kit list'. Mountain equipment like warm clothes, rain gear and snacks for your expedition. If you don't want to carry much over to Tanzania, company staff will direct you to stores in Tanzania where you can hire them.

Finally, on accommodation, the company probably have an associated hotel or will suggest some for you in Arusha or Moshi. Choose the hotel that you want and remember everything will be included except tipping!

Chapter 6 – Routes up the Kilimanjaro

Getting to the mountain:

In total, there are seven paths up the mountain, but five of these are for ascent only. You are not allowed to descend using these trails. Marangu route is open for both. Mweka is a descent only.

The six ascent trails leading up to the foot of Kibo peak, run anti-clockwise beginning with the Western most trails, the little used Shira Plateau route, Lemosho route, Machame route, Umbwe route, Marangu route and running from the North-Eastern side, the Rongai (Loitoktok) route. These six routes eventually meet a path circling the Kibo cone, a path known as a either the northern or the southern circuit depending on which side of mountain you are.

Stage one - Rongai Gate to Simba campsite - distance 7km, altimeter 2635m - time 2-3 hours

The Rongai route is on the north side of Kilimanjaro, which borders Loitokitoki town in Kenya, some fifteen minutes from the gate and is also the only route where you have good chance of seeing animals. On this route you can trek from five to seven days, but seven days is recommended. Climb for five days to third cave and then the route joins at Kibo basecamp (not recommend). This climb could also start in Kenya at Loitokitoki subject to having correct permit.

Stage one - Rongai gate to Simba camp - distance 7km, altimeter 2635m - time 2-3 hours

With registration completed at the gate, you may also wish to have lunch in the tourist shelter behind the office. The trek begins with a walk through the Pine plantation, where the local villagers grow Irish Potatoes, Maize and Beans. Soon after, you'll turn into the Rain Forest where you may see elephants, blue Monkeys, black and white Colobus and dick dick? Eventually, the forest gives way to heath land, where you can see giant heathers and St. John's Worts at the camp.

Stage two - Simba camp to Kikelelwa - distance 12km, altimeter 3675m - time 6-7 hours

A steep climb through the moorland up to lunch point (the second cave). Post lunch, a gradual anticlockwise route to Kikelelwa. The plants on this journey are Gladioli, Red hot Poker and Caduskenonsiss.

Also, Cenesio Kilimanjari and Giant Lobelia welcome you to the camp.

Stage three - Kikelelwa camp to Mawenzi turn hut
distance 3.5 km,
altimeter 4302km
time 3-4 hours

Whilst it's a short day, it's a steep walk from moorland to the Alpine desert. Surprisingly, the camp is surrounded by small lakes. Plants here are the Everlasting flower, Giant Lobelia and Cenicio Kilimanjari

Stage four - Mawenzi turn hut altimeter 4302m

An extra day at Mawenzi turn hut for acclimatisation around the peak.

Stage five - Mawenzi turn hut to Kibo hut - distance 10 km, altimeter 4714m time - 4-5 hours

Return down path for 10 minutes, then turn left and continue to Kibo along the saddle. The trail is gradual until the lunch point then uphill. With lunch consumed, head to the camp. The only plant found here is the Yellow Everlasting.

Stage six - The Summit - distance 6km altimeter 5895m - time 6 hours
Departure for the summit is at midnight. Mountain top is in three parts. A sand rock start and from Gillman point, a walk on the crater rim. Finally, at Stella Point is the glacier on the side with the volcanic ash pit.

After climbing it, you have to come down! The descent is on the Marangu route via Horombo and the Mandara camp

The Marangu Route:

Due to its popularity, it is commonly referred to as the Coca-Cola trail! Trekkers pick this route because as the walk is only five or six days, they think that the climb to the summit will be easy. However, a huge fact here is that a greater proportion of people fail on this route than any other.

One of the reasons why people believe that the Marangu route is easier is because of the existence of sleeping huts. My own experience (as a lead guide on the mountain) is that sleeping in huts is more difficult than sleeping in tents. With huts, there is lack of oxygen, not enough space to fully stretch your body whilst sleeping and cannot sit upright without bending. Tents might give you some irritation with stones on the ground but they are nothing in comparison to huts. Nobody has their own room (sometimes four, six or eight share) and these others could be from different companies. You simply wake up tired.

In addition, at Horombo, this is like a motorway junction as people here share rooms with those who are coming down the mountain. They will want to celebrate! You don't!

The accommodation in the huts must be booked in advance by your tour company as they have to pay a deposit per person per night to Kilimanjaro National Park in order to secure it. You may also be asked for a deposit too.

Stage one: Marangu Gate - Mandara Hut.
Distance: 8 kms
Altitude: 1905m/6250ft -:2723m/8934ft
Time: 3-4 Hours

2 hours driving from Arusha and 45 minutes from Moshi, Registration is done at the gate and the process usually takes an hour or more depending on the number of the tourists on the day.

Your walk begins by following the trekker's path, which heads left of the road whilst the road is used by the porters. The Rain forest will present itself as you continue uphill. You might be lucky to see a troop of blue Monkeys or black and white Colobus although they are shy.

The Impatiens Kilimanjaro the small flowers you'll see (that has almost become the emblem of Kilimanjaro) and after approximately an hour and half, you'll find a bridge that leads the trail to the right hand side where the Kisambioni picnic area stands. Here you join a rough broken road (porter trail) where you will eat lunch. This is half way to Mandara.

Back on the road again, continue climbing north to the small waterfall. Five minutes from here the trails join together. From here to the Mandara, both Porter and hikers share. The trail gets steeper here, but this is set off by the natural beauty. The first appearance of the giant heather along with masses of border lichens, welcomes you to Mandara huts at 2723m. The huts are comprised of small rooms and one large dormitory in the roof above the dining room.

Fifteen minutes away from Mandara huts is the parasitic cone known as the Maundi crater and is worth visiting for the wild flowers and grass growing on its slopes. Good views here of Kenya, Lake Chala, Nyumba ya Mungu and north west to Mawenzi. On your way to the crater, look on the branches of the trees as you may see tree Hyracks and also Monkeys.

The Mandara hut was named after the name of the Moshi chief whom perceived to be a fearsome warrior.

Stage two: Mandara hut to Horombo huts.
Distance: 12.5 kms
Altitude: 3721m/12,208feet
Time: 5-6 hours

Fifteen minutes walk from your hut and the forest is left behind as you now walk through Moorland. There are good views of the twin peaks Mawenzi and Kibo.

As you continue to climb, the peak becomes larger and clear (if weather permits). Tall grass becomes the order of the day but look out for the unique Senecio Kilimanjaro and Lobelia Deckini.

Thirty minutes away from the sloping bridge is a picnic area where you can stop for lunch. This is probably half way to Horombo. Thereafter, the journey is approx one and a half hours to two. A gradual uphill walk

Horombo hut (3721m) is a big camp with small huts for four to six people and large huts for 16 people+. Food is provided via two dining halls and can accommodate people who are coming down from the mountain and those who are going up. Because people taking six days to ascend will stay an extra day for acclimatisation, this makes the camp the busiest on the mountain.

If you are taking six days, then you are acclimatising yourself at Zebra rock or higher at Mawenz hut on the northern upper route to Kibo.

Stage three: Horombo to Kibo hut via lower route
Distance: 9.5 Kms

Altitude: 4714m/15,466ft
Time: 4-5 hours

The path from Horombo now divides into two: the southern (lower route) and the northern (upper route).

The northern route is usually taken by climbers whom have already acclimatized. The southern route whilst begins steeply, it calms down and if you intend to take this route (and don't want to take time acclimatizing), ask your guide to take the northern route on the return leg, so that you are familiar with both routes.

Walking up through thick moorland vegetation and after thirty minutes you arrive at the Maua river (3914m). The terrain climbs steadily post Maua, continue to walk past the Southern section to the lost water point well the sing point and the picnic table. Commence the uphill approach to the Mawenzi ridge, beyond that you will see the 'Saddle' with the red hill in the middle and a large parasitic cone to the right. The trail becomes flat here and is extremely wind swept and dramatic.

Continue northwards across the Saddle to Jiwe la Ukoyo, a former campsite where trekkers stop for lunch. It is also the meeting point between the two paths from Horombo. From here to Kibo is easily an hour and quarter and despite the huts looking close, it's a tough walk.

The stone building (Kibo huts) welcomes you. On the door, there is a sign that tells you that you are now at 4750m.

Stage four : Kibo hut to Uhuru peak.
Distance: 6.25km
Altimeter: 5895m/19,341ft
Time: 6 hours
At around midnight, hikers start to walk 'Pole Pole' (baby steps) from Kibo huts directly to the summit. After one hour and forty five minutes you pass the Williaus point, usually the first resting point where you can unzip your jackets if it's hot or add more if it's cold. Thirty minutes further on and you arrive at Hans Mayer cave where the Hungarian hunter Samuel Tereki rested in 1887.

The climbing becomes tougher now as the path steepens, so the zigzag walking begins from the Hans Meyer cave all the way up to Jamaica rocks where most of trekkers give up. You will undoubtedly be breathless the whole way up from this point, but don't worry it's a short walk at one hour.

Arrive at Gillimas point and rest for a few minutes. Congratulate yourself at this point because the hike from Gillimas to Stella point is nothing but a walk around the crater rim. At Stella point you will meet other walkers from Barafu.

Finally, enjoy the sunrise and the view of Mawenzi peak on your back. The time to Uhuru peak is just forty five minutes and you climb between the glaciers on your left side and desolate enormity of the crater on your right. At the top, you will find the sign congratulating you. On your left (in front) is the view of her sister mountain (Meru).

The Shira Plateau and the Lemoshoe.

The Lemoshoe route

These two treks have been put together and go across the Shira Plateau. Hikers should obtain their valid permit at Londrosi gate where the 2 trails separate, the Shira plateau goes straight and the Lemoshoe route turns left. The trail combines again at the Shira

.

To find the Londrosi gate, drive from Arusha or Moshi to Boma ya Ng'ombe. Continue to Sanya Juu rod through to Ngare village/Nairobi and Samba form. Keep travelling west to Kilimanjaro forest plantation gate, make your payment for crossing the forest plantation to Londorosi gate.

NOTE: If you have driven a long way, note that Shira camp one is 30 minutes from the starting point on the Shira plateau route.

The Lemoshoe route.
This and the Rongai route were the last trails to be discovered and they were found by following poacher's trails. Due to its wealth of nature, it makes it very popular for visitors. Lots of both flora and fauna, (largely thanks to its proximity to both Amboseli National Park in Kenya) and the west Kilimanjaro wildlife corridor, from where herds of Elephants, Eland, Buffalo, Jackos and big cats such as Leopard can be seen. In days gone by, trekkers on this trail were accompanied by park rangers to protect them from dangerous animals,
This trail takes seven to eight days though some walkers take nine to ten days.

Stage one: Londoros Gate to Mti Mkubwa big tree camp.
Distance: 5km
Altimeter: 2785m/9137ft
Time: 3-4 hours
Post permit purchase and luggage weigh in, drive one hour through the forest plantation. This large plantation is owned by the Government and managed under Tanzania natural resources and tourism Ministry. On occasions, the farmers allowed to grow their own food. Irish potatoes, carrots and green beans are very popular which are mostly sold in Arusha town. At the end of rough track road, you'll see the hiking signs from here to Mti Mkubwa/big tree camp. You'll walk through the rain forest while spotting Monkey, both colours, flowers like impatient Kilimanjaro and pseudo viola.

The forest camp lies at the top of the ridge in the Sghad of a wonderful Podocaipus and African night accompanied by the noise of Colours, Turaco and Tree Hiraxs.

Stage two: Mti Mkubwa/big tree-Shira one camp.
Distance: 8kms
Altimeter: 3504m/11,496ft
Time: 5-6 hours

Hope you are now familiar with the flora and fauna. Just 40 minutes walk from the forest to the moorland. Here you will have a good view of the Ngare Nairobi. Keep your climb 'Pole Pole', through the moorland and uphill to the lunch point. The steepness continues with the view of the rough track road on the Shira plateau route. You are now at Mgongo wa Tembo (elephant back) as the ridge looks like an Elephant's backend.

The path becomes steep and challenging, so 'Pole Pole' to the top of the ridge (network point for mobile phones). Most of trekkers stop here and check their inbox and text. Here the height is around 3536m above sea level. The Shira ridge is to your right, snow-capped Kibo ahead and the plateau at your feet. As you ascend higher you eventually arrive at Shira one campsite at 3504m. Populous here are Steaky seed eaters, Alpine Chat and four Stripped Mice.

Stage three: Shira one - Shira hut
Distance: 7kms
Altimeter: 3,895m/12,779ft
Time: 4-5 hours

The Lemoshoe and the Shiraplateu routes cross here on their way to Shira camp. The first one is heads North West (South East back) across the plateau. The second is via the Cathedral on the Plateau (Southern) and is mostly used for acclimatization, climbing up to 3862m before dropping again.

Some trekkers head straight to Moir hut on the Westside of Kibo instead of going to the camp at Shira two. These are long treks on the mountain of between 8-10 days.

Shira one to shira two. Take the regular route across the plateau, which is very popular for Buffalo and other animals like Eland, Klip Springer and Dikdik who cross the plateau in search of mineral salt and fresh grass. Cross the rough road from the Shira plateau route to Samba cave 3640m. The cave sits North East of the junction and has toilets nearby.

Walk another 40 minutes to the top of the ridge were the trail separates. One way goes to Shira two camp and another one goes left to Moir huts via

Fisha camp. The Fisha camp was discovered by an American mountaineer known as Scott Fisherr, whom was clearly a mountain madman. He died at base camp trying to rescue his group. The Shira two camp lies 35 minutes from the junction 3895m. This camp is very close to Shira cave camp via the Machame route.

Stage four: Shira two huts – Barronco camp via Lava tower
Distance: 10km
Altimeter: 3986m/13077ft
Time: 6 -7hours

Onward to Lava tower. Barren Alpine desert, heather and moorland all in one. Over your right shoulder is mount Meru. If you look on the floor, you will see shining black obsidian/black diamonds.

From Shira two to Lava tower is about 6.5kms. You head uphill and then flattens out and crosses the gateway to the Moor hut, which is 30 minutes away. Popular short break and photo spot to take your time.

When ready again, head South to the top of the ridge where the junction to Machame route is. 20 minutes later, the path on the left is shortcut to Barranco, mostly used by the porters. Unless you are staying the night at Lava Tower, move onto the path loop heading South East and it divides into two. One goes down the Barranco and the other heads to the summit, know as the Western Breach route.

Branch off east towards the Lava tower. Descend from 4627m to 3986m. Barranco is squeezed between Kibo and the Tower itself and continues downhill for circa 2 hours to Barranco. Look out for the endemic plants that grow on the available water. From here, the follow path across the Barranco wall to the top of it and it's only 45 minutes to the camp at Malakite.

Look out for Sun bird's fling from one plant to another and from those endemic plants, a little forest of Senisio welcomes you to the camp.

Stage five: Barranco hut - Barafu camp
Distance: 8.5 kms
Altimeter: 4662m/15,295ft
Time: 6-7 hours

The great Barranco Wall is indeed a beautiful but imposing sight. Sometimes, during the night in the tent, you wonder how you would ever scale it. Many questions get asked about this huge wall, but I can assure you it is very easy and you are in no need of rope.

To begin, walk through the rocks and you begin the climb. Use your hands to pull yourself up where needed. 'Jiwe la Kubusu' (kissed stone) is the name give to a stone that you have to hug to get around it. Exercise care here.

After two hours rock climbing, you finally reach the top. You get a clear view of mount Meru and of Kibo behind you. You are now above the clouds and it's good place to snap some pictures, drink water and snack!, After your break is finished, take out your walking poles for the downhill that follows.

After 40 minutes or so, you'll encounter another uphill. Continue to use your walking poles, especially those with knee problems. Another uphill walk to the top of the ridge where you can see Karanga camp, the path to Barafu and the Millennium. It looks very close, but you are still one hour to Karanga camp. Of that, 30 minutes downhill to the Karanga valley and 40 minutes uphill through the valley.

Karanga camp is at 3930m. Some trekkers stop at this point for lunch then proceed to Barafu camp. Those who have more than seven days break stay over night at this camp, which is recommended, as you have more time to rest before you attempt the summit.

Stage six: Barafu Camp - Uhuru peak.
Distance: 6 kms
Altimeter: 5895m/19,341ft
Time: 6 hrs
It's now time to take your place on the top of Africa. From the first day to here, you will have done a lot of walking and enjoyed seeing lots of different flora and fauna. Now, you come to the hardest thing you have done in your life.

On this last climb, you don't need to carry a lot of stuff, so make your backpack lighter. Only carry, candy, cookies, energy bars, sunglasses, sun-cream and three or four litres of water and some pain killers.

This final stage begins at the midnight and consists of three sections. First is the rocky part, which actually begins from Barafu camp. Section two, Cossovo to Stella Point is sand and part rocks. Section three is Stella point to Uhuru peak and is 45 minutes to 1 hour.

Arrival at Uhuru peak. Congratulate yourself. On way down to Barafu, make sure you take the right path from the peak otherwise you will find yourself at Kibo camp.

Umbwe Route

Stage one: Umbwe gate – Umbwe care
Distance: 9.6km
Altitude: 2,944 m/9,656ft
Time: 5-6 hours
Drive along the Moshi to Arusha road until you reach Barabara ya Kibosho, then turn right into Kibosho road. Head North on Marram road, pass the Banana cultivation and coffee fields you soon reach Umbwe gate. Registration and weigh up of luggage complete, the hike begins with a walk through the forest while enjoying the scenery, bird calls and the Colobus travelling from tree to tree.

Two hours later, the 4 x4 road ends and the Umbwe trail begins. The path heads North/Northeast and the soil lessens so you walk on the roots of trees. After I hour or so, through the dense forest, you arrive at the lunch point, where you will see the marvellous Umbwe river. Then join the ridge again, which will take you to camp

.

Stage two: Umbwe cave – Barranco huts
Distance: 4.75km
Altimeter: 3,986m/13,077ft
Time 5-6 hours

The second stage of Umbwe is walking away from the forest to heather and moorland. The climbing here is more challenging as it is uphill all the way. There may be times when you need to use rope 'Jiwe la Kamba' (in other words rope rock), but if you haven't got any, then don't worry, it's not a problem. The trail is uphill all the way and so you could be forgiven not to notice flowers like Gladiolus Watsonides, red-hot pokers and Helichysums.

From Jiwe la Kambago, proceed on the North wad and soon the heather begins to disappear as does the grass. Continue your climb North towards the Barancoridge. You start climb again before heading off right to the camp. It's the second day for you, but the third day for those from Machame and the fourth for those from Lemoshoe.

Stage three: Barranco huts - Lava Tower
Distance : 3kms
Altimeter: 4,627m/15,180ft
Time: 3-4 hours

While other climbers head to Barafu via Karanga camp, your route is uphill via the Barranco valley to the Lava Tower. Five minutes into the walk you pass by a small forest of Senisio Kilimanjaro, the oldest specimen on the mountain. You can work out its age by counting its branches. Also, the Lobelia is here and the Malkait sunbird flies from plant to plant.

A while into the journey and you find yourself on a gentle trail which then turns steeply up to Lava tower, Lunch time!

Stage four: Lava Tower - Arrow Glacier/the western branch.
Distance: 2.5km
Altimeter: 4,871m/15,081ft
Time: 3-4 hours

It may be the shortest route but it is also the steepest! Worryingly, the trail is subject to frequent rock falls and there are some places your guide will stop and listen out for any heading in your direction. In January 2000, three American climbers perished in a rockslide near Arrow Glacier. After the accident, the Kilimanjaro National Park established some legislation to regulate safety on this route. All hikers on this route must now wear helmets and sign disclaimers.

Trekkers like to take this risky route to explore the crater, Ash pit, Furtwangler Glacier and other features of the summit. If snow has fallen over the trail, then an ice axe may be required.

The hike begins by crossing the stream that flows below the Lava tower, before climbing steeply in a South East direction to the top of the ridge before descending down again for a few seconds. Then proceed to the second ridge (heading eastward) to the Arrow Glacier campsite - although it's the steepest, you can make this in one hour.

Stage five: **Arrow Glacier – Uhuru**
Distance: 3 km
Altimeter: 5,895m/19,341ft
Time: 4 hours.

If you are sick at this camp there is no way to return down immediately. You will have to return to the crater and then descend via Stella to Barafu camp. Assuming you are ok, walk for some minutes towards the crater rim with the Furtwangler Glacier on your left, past campsite then begin climbing to Uhuru peak. Take the path up to the Reusch crater and Ash pit viewpoint.

After the summit you will descend via Stella point to Barafu camp, then proceed to Mweka camp for an overnight stay.

The Machame Route

The Machame Route is known as the Whisky route. Holds a very high success rate for the hikers reaching the top, more than any other trail on the mountain. This trail allows trekkers to acclimatize better than any other.

The trail is oldest trail on the mountain and is very popular. Trekkers usually take 6 days or 7 days on this trail but 7 days is highly recommended On this trail you can able to summit via he Western breach or Barafu.

The trail is home to various species of animals and birds but the most common is the Monkey Also, there are some animals that very rare to see like Jackal, Tree Hiracks and Leopards. Birds like Turco, Raven, Sunbird, Mouse bird, Tropical Boubau and many others too. The floras here are Impatiens Kilimanjari Lobelias, Sensio Fireball lily and Hychresium.

The journey begins on the South Western side of the mountain, walking through the cultivated area to the Rain Forest, past Heath and Moorland, along the Alpine desert to the summit.

Stage one: Machame Gate - Machame hut

Distance: 10.75Km
Altimeter: 3,000m
Time: 4 - 5 hours.

Driving from Moshi town, turn right before the Kwasadala River and continue along the Machame road. Passing through Machame village where the locals grow Bananas, Cassaa, Coffee and Maize. After 45 minutes or so, you reach the gate where your guides or travel agency organise a valid permit and registration occurs.

The walk begins by following the 4x4 road for 40 or so minutes. The walk now takes you into dense forest, where you can pick up on the bird calls. The flowers here Fire ball lily, Impaction. Kilimanjari Paveta and so many others.

After hiking for 2 hours and 30 minutes (approx) you'll be at almost half way for the day, you'll find some toilets and old trees laying down where you can stop for lunch and use the old trees as chairs and tables (this is a natural picnic site).
The hike continues along the forest floor, catch the stream running down on your right hand side. Starting now to get a bit uphill, the forest begins to disappear and the Heather Ericas emerge. Within a few minutes you'll find yourself at the camp with a sign post showing the altimeter of where you are at..

Stage two: Machame Hut – Shera cave
Distance: 5.3km
Altimeter: 3839m/12, 595ft
Time: 4-5 hours

Day 2 begins with a short steep walk through the dense heather and Ericas covered by bearded lichens, through the rocks until you reach the top of the ridge, where you can see Shira plateau. Take a short break for 15 – 20 minutes for water and to take pictures.

The climb continues through the moorland all the way to the camp. After a long hike you arrive at the top of the second ridge where there is a big rock/stone and some hikers climb to the top of the rock for a great view of Kobo in the front and Meru behind. I hour and 30 minutes from the rock is lunch point. Once there Mice and Ravens will wait for your scraps. It is highly recommended that you don't feed them or any species on the park as you interfere with nature.

From the lunch point, continue left and it's less steep now. Just climb to the top of the ridge then walk on the flat to the camp. Look out for obsidian rock all over, from the top of the ridge all the way to camp. After you cross the stream the camp is upon you with a ranger hut and one of the better toilets on the mountain.

At Shira two campsite, you are twenty minutes west from Shira cave. Also West is Shira Cathedral and Shira hill overlooking Meru.

Stage 3: Shira cave – Barranco huts via Lava Tower
Distance: 10.75km
Altimeter: 3,975m/13,077 ft
Time: 6-7 hours

The climb begins with a gentle but steady walk through the Alpine desert to the Western slopes of Kibo. The Lava tower houses different species of birds and flowers like Alpine Chak, Ravens and also everlasting flowers.

After hiking for about 2 and a half hours you arrive at the top of the ridge where you might also meet with the trekkers from Lemoshoe and the Shira plateau. From here to the Lava Tower is approximately 2 hours but before you reach it, the trail diverts into two. The Lava Tower trail and the porters trail, the shortcut to Barranco.

The Lava Tower is a vertical protrusion of volcanic rock poking sky ward. Here you can have lunch. On completion, walk another 1 hour and 30 minutes down hill to Barranco moving from Alpine to moorland and 30 minutes from the small water fall is the Barranco camp with a ranger post and smart toilets. This camp on the mountain can accommodate climbers from 4 different routes.

Stage four: Barranco hut – Barafu CAMP
Distance: 8.5km

Altimeter: 4,634m
Time: 5-6 hours

Day 4 begins with a big hike up the great Barranco wall... to the top of it and then down the Karanga valley. At the top of Karanga camp, stop for lunch and then continue to Barafu camp for your midnight summit attempt. Most of the travel companies recommend a seven day excursion on this route, so you can stay overnight at Karanga camp before continuing to Barafu camp.

Stage five: Barafu camp - Uhuru peak.
Distance: 4.86km
Altimeter: 5,895m/19.342ft
Time: 5 – 6 hours

The summit attempt begins during the night walking 'pole pole' to Uhuru via Stella point then the descending via the Mweka route.

The Mweka Route

As mentioned earlier in the book, there are only 2 routes for descending Kili. This is one of them. All other routes must be adhered to unless there is an emergency event like a wild fire. In 2013, along the Mandara, all the way up near Horombo, there was a wild fire, which led trekkers to take the Rongai route as a temporary route.

The Mweka route is the descent for Machame route and has two stages.

Stage one: Uhuru peak to Mweka hut.
Distance: **11km**
Altimeter: **3**
Time:

After being at the roof of Africa, its time to return. The descent from the top to Uhuru is quite a challenge as its steep downhill. Trekkers make it back to Barafu between 2 – 4 hours. It depends on your fitness and strength, but also your joints e.g. knees.

To go all the way down would take until morning. When you arrive at Barafu camp, stop for a break and reduce your clothes if you haven't done so already.

Pack your stuff and say bye to Barafu camp, some trekkers need extra time to lie down before continuing to Mweka. However, is recommended to descend to a lower altitude to avoid mountain sickness. The descent from the summit is via the Alpine desert, then heather and moorland. Mweka camp lies a few metres from the rain forest.

Stage two: Mweka camp/ hut – Mweka gate.
Distance: **9km**
Altimeter: **1633m**
Time: **2 – 3 hours.**

A new day brings less pain now and the tiredness also begins to disappear. Descend through the rainforest, enjoying the bird calls and the quietness of the forest.

2 hours later, you'll find yourself at the 4 x 4 road the 30 minutes further, you'll be at the gate ready for signing out. Your vehicle should be there waiting for you, ready to deliver you to your hotel and that bath or shower you've been craving.

The Marangu Route

Distance:
Altimeter:
Time:

This route supports ascent and descent. The reason for that? This was the first route to be discovered, thus all activities were engaged here. Is the descent route of the Pongai route and Marangu.

Some believe that the Marangu route is easer because a shorter trail (measured by distance) and because you sleep in relative comfort i.e. in huts. My own experience as a leading guide on the mountain is that this route has a 'high fail rate' due to its steepness and less opportunity to acclimatize. My advice for those who wish to take this route; take enough exercise before attempting it. If possible, begin with Mount Meru (4,565m) to acclimatize first.

Stage one: Uhuru – Horombo hut.
Distance:
Altimeter:
Time:

The descent begins from Uhuru along Gilman's point to Kibo. Then it's steep downhill on the trail. As its sandy, most of trekkers slide down but this route is for those with good knees.

After Kibo, proceed along the saddle with strong winds all the way down through the Moorland to the Horombo camp.

Stage two: Horombo hut – Marangu gate
Distance: 19km
Altimeter: 1905m
Time: 5 – 6 hours.

The Marangu is the longest route down, so, you will easily spend more than 5 hours to the gate via the Mandara hut.

From Mandara, walk through the forest to the gate. Sign out, drive along the cultivated area to the hotel for shower and overnight sleep.

Chapter 7 - Illness and Rescue

Whatever your reason for the expedition is, you must have fun. You will automatically experience many emotions like happiness, joy, sadness or despair and realities like pain or disease and of course a different culture. During your stay you might end up feeling ill, so it is important to give you the tips about the common ailments walkers face and what to do about them.

Mountain Sickness

The human body functions, best at sea level in a temperate climate. So, at higher altitudes, your body will naturally be under pressure unless familiarisation has occurred (acclimatization). An individual normally resident at sea level whom ascends above 3000 metres may experience various uncomfortable symptoms. These include headache, nausea, breathlessness on slight exertion palpitations, undue fatigue and a feeling of heaviness in the muscles. All these symptoms subside in the course of the first week as the body acclimatizes to the lower oxygen pressure.

There are two more serious forms of mountain sickness but these are seldom seen in southern Africa because of the absence of really high mountains (over 5000 mitres). Congestion of the lungs (high – altitude pulmonary Oedema) causes extreme breathlessness, a dry hacking cough, chest pain and palpitations. Congestion of the brain (high – altitude cerebral dema) causes severe headache, vomiting, and visual impairment whilst walking. Both conditions can be fatal and it is essential that the victim move to a lower altitude as quickly as possible.

How to avoid it?

Mountain sickness can be avoided by:

1. Climbing to high altitudes in planned stages.
2. Avoiding over exertion for the first few days when entering a new altitude.
3. Taking plenty of rest. The acclimatization process is enhanced by taking Acetazelamide tablets (Diamox) in the morning. This will increase the flow of urine and so counteract fluid retention. Spend nights at the lowest possible altitude consistent with the expedition objectives.

A climber who continues to experience unpleasant symptoms after three of four days should descend to a lower altitude and allow symptoms to subside completely.

Ankle injuries

Ankle   injuries occur when sudden twisting force is applied to the joint, for example, slipping   on loose gravel or wet   grass. Damage to the ligaments may cause blood or fluid into cavities and cause rapid swelling.

If the ligaments surrounding the ankle have merely been stretched (sprained), any movement of the joint is likely to cause discomfort. Solution is to rest over a number of days. However, if ligaments have been torn, seek medical treatment immediately.

The injured joint should be bandaged tightly and elevated on a cushion or some other support. Codeine or Paracetamol tablets will relieve pain.

Blisters

Foot care is an of utmost importance during any hike or walking tour. To avoid blisters, socks should be thick and boots should be worn in and comfortable.

The advice is to stop at the first feeling of friction so that footwear can be adjusted and chafed areas of skin covered with plasters before   blistering occurs. If a blister occurs, it should be left intact. Cover liberally with plasters as this reduces the chance of infection. Blisters reabsorb over several days but large blisters may need to be pricked using a sterile needle, then   cover with micropose and several plasters.

At the end of the day, your feet should be washed and plasters renewed.

Dislocated joints

Dislocation of a joint is commonly associated with the stretching or rupture of surrounding ligaments. The joints most commonly dislocated are: shoulder, hip, ankle, the small joint of the finger or thumb. The joint may appear deformed and will soon become swollen.

What to do

Dislocation of a finger joint can often be reduced by applying gentle pressure to the distal end of the finger, which should then be supported by strapping it to an adjacent finger. Fractures, obstruction or tearing of arteries should be   left in the place which causes the least amount of discomfort and held by a crepe bandage. Painkillers are a good idea too!

Chest pain

Chest pain can be the result of a serious cardiac event, or it could be from less serious problems such as broken rib or respiratory infection. Use PAS to determine the cause.

Risk Factors:
Family or personal history of heart problems, increasing age especially in males. High cholesterol, high blood pressure, sedentary lifestyle, smoking, diabetes, or obesity.

Signs and symptoms:
Chest pain, chest tightness or pressure, pain radiating to the jaw and left arm. Weakness, dizziness, light-headedness, nausea, vomiting. Indigestion and heartburn. Women and men present different symptoms, so watch out for shortness of breath too.

Treatment includes:
Evacuation and 'Advanced Life attention', if needed. Certainly rest, make comfortable, reassure, positive pressure ventilation, use medication that they may carry and if needed oxygen. As a general rule, patients should not walk on/back unless their chest pain has resolved.

Asthma

Asthma is a respiratory condition involving the bronchial tubes in the lungs, which can be life-threatening. Many factors can bring on an attack, including pollen, animal hair, certain foods, upper respiratory infections, emotional stress, exercise, or exposure to cold air.

During an acute attack, the muscles around the small breathing tubes in the lungs tighten or constrict, causing wheezing, coughing and the sensation of not being able to get enough breath in. Other symptoms of a severe attack include bluish tinge to the lips and fingers, rapid heartbeat, gasping for air and confusion.

Treatment
Breathing medications, which contain bronchodilators. They should always use their own prescribed medicines. The victim should be evacuated to a medical facility as soon as possible.

Back pain

Back pain ranks among the top 10 most common ailments in backpackers. The lower part of the back takes most of the weight of the body and is therefore more likely to give you problems. Preventing a back injury is a lot easier than trying to recover from one. While on the trail, there are several things you can do to lessen the chances of injuring your back.

Prevention

- Stretch before lifting your pack, especially in the morning when the muscles are cold and stiff.
-When putting on heavy pack, keep your back straight and in a neutral position. S
- If necessary, put your pack on the floor and slip one shoulder into a loosened shoulder strap. Roll the pack onto your back and use your legs, not your back and arms, to lift yourself up.
- When lifting, always keep objects close to the body.
- Adjust the pack so as much weight as possible is on the hip belt, instead of the shoulder straps.
- Use a walking stick for added balance and support.

Although back pain may be a symptom of a more serious condition, it is often due to strained muscles.

Treatment

If possible, lie on your back with a pillow under your knees or on your side with a pillow between your legs for one to two days before resuming gentle and graded activity.

Extended bed rest and inactivity can actually weaken the back and delay recovery. Most people with sudden back pain will recover completely within two to four weeks.

Other treatment

- Anti-inflammatory medication such as Ibuprofen (if allowed)
- Application of cold compresses
- Gentle massage.

Diarrhea

Diarrhea is an increase in the frequency and looseness of stools.

Causes of diarrhea include virus, bacteria, parasites, (such as Giardia or Cryptosporidium), food allergies, inflammatory bowel disease and anxiety.

A major concern with diarrhea is the amount of fluid loss or dehydration that results. The degree of dehydration can be estimated from certain signs and symptoms:

- Mild dehydration [3% to 5% weight loss] thirst, tacky mucous membranes on lips and mouth, a normal pulse, and finally dark urine.
- Moderate dehydration (5% to 10% weight loss) thirst, dry mucous membranes, sunken eyes, small volume of dark urine, rapid and weak pulse.
- Severe dehydration (greater than 10% weight loss) drowsiness or lethargy, very dry mucous membranes, sunken eyes, no urine, no tears, shock (a rapid pulse or one that is difficult to feel).

General treatment

1. Replace lost fluids and Electrolytes.

Oral rehydration with both water and salts is the most important treatment for diarrhea illness. The fluids and electrolytes lost through diarrhea can be potentially fatal in children and devastating in adults too. The body has the ability to absorb the water and electrolytes given orally, even during a severe bout of diarrhea.

Diarrhea contains Sodium Chloride (salt), Potassium and Bicarbonate. Drinking plain water is an inadequate replacement. Many sport drinks sold commercially are not ideal replacements for diarrhea losses because the high concentration of sugar may increase fluid loss and the electrolyte contents may not be optimal. Gatorade can be used, but should be diluted to half-strength with water.

The World Health Organization recommends oral rehydration solutions that contain the following combination of electrolytes added to one litre of water: sodium chloride 3.5g, potassium chloride 1.5 g, glucose 20g and sodium bicarbonate 2.5g.

2. Anti-poop drugs

If the victim does not have bloody diarrhea or a fever greater than 101 degrees Fahrenheit Imodium can be taken orally to reduce cramping and diarrhea. The dose for adults is 4 mg initially, followed by 2 mg after each loose bowel movement up to a maximum of 14 mg per day.

Imodium is preferred over Lomotil because it has fewer potential side effects. Imodium should not be given to children. Pepto-Bismol or Kaopectate are other commonly used anti-motility drugs and may be helpful.

3. Antibiotics.

Antibiotics are recommended if the diarrhea is accompanied by fever of 101 F or greater, or, if there is pus or blood in the stool, or, if the victim has signs and symptoms of Giardiasis .

Note, medicines should only be given if you are not allergic to them.

Getting down from the Mountain
There are three ways to evacuate the patient from the mountain:
- Flying doctors; in serious conditions this will be recommended, which will require travel insurance.
- Stretchers; also know as 'The Kilimanjaro Express'. These are dotted around the park, already covered in the park fees. The stretchers can be used in places where the 4x4 cannot access.
- 4x4 vehicles.
- Walk down, if the patient is well enough.

Chapter 8 - Mount Meru

Introduction

Mt Meru is a dormant stratovolcano located 70 Kilometers (43 miles) west of mount Kilimanjaro in northern Tanzania at the height of 4,565 metres, which makes it the fifth highest mountain in Africa. It is visible from Mt Kilimanjaro on clear day and that's why they call them sisters.

Trekking to the peak of Mt Meru can be done from three to four days, though four days are highly recommended. Meru is among the major activities in Arusha National park, other activities include:

- Game drive in the park where there is a well organized road network east of Momela, including the lakes and the rim of the Ngurudoto crater,
- Canoeing at the small Momela lake
- Walking safaris.

Flora and fauna

The mountains lying at the heart of Arusha National Park offer a wide variety of habitats. Typical animals include: Colobus, Monkey, Blue Monkey, Warthog, Buffalo, Giraffe, Elephant, Dik Dik, Bushbuck, Suni, and some of the predator's that very rare to see like Leopards and Hyena.

Almost 450 bird species have been recorded in the park

The Route

There are two paths that head for the first camp at Miriakamba, namely the southern and northern route. From this camp, one path takes you all the way to the top.

The southern route is the most popular route [4x4 road] and takes 5 hours to reach Miriakamba. By taking this route, you will acclimatize yourself on the first day, which increases the possibility of conquering the summit.

On the last day, you will have advantage of taking the other path on the northern route [a shortcut] that crosses the middle on an open glade.

Day 1- Momela – Miriakamba
Elevation: 1,597 m- 2, 500 m
Distance: 13 km
Time: 5 hours

Drive either from Arusha or Moshi to Momela Gate. After a short registration, the walk begins with a ranger in front escorting you. Easy to spot wild animals including Giraffe, Buffalo, Zebras, Monkeys and many others.

Dinner and overnight at Miriakamba.

Day 2 Miriakamba – saddle hut
Elevation: 2,500 m- 3,500 m
Distance: 6 km
Time: 4 hours

The walk from Miriakamba Hut to the saddle (below little Meru) is a short day but a steep climb. The walk then takes you slowly along the ridge for a spectacular view of the Meru crater and the impressive ash cone.

After a hot lunch at the saddle hut, the short climb to little Meru [3,820m] is followed with a superb view of the sunset. Dinner and short rest for about 5 hours before the summit.

Day 3 Summit – Miriakamba
Elevation: 3,500m -4,565m and down to 2,500m
Distance : 16 km
Time : 3 hours

Early at around 8:00 am, you start to the summit. Climb steeply to Rhino Point [3,800m] and on to Cobra Point [4350 m] . Reach the summit [4,565 m] by sunrise. There is a possibility of seeing Kilimanjaro peak above the clouds.

The final part of the climb is along a spectacular narrow ridge between the sheer inner cliffs and the sloping outer wall of the crater. A short rest here and have lunch at the saddle hut before starting descending down to Miriakamba for dinner and overnight.

Day 4 Miriakamba to Momela gate
Elevation
Distance 7km
Time

A short and fast descent via open grassland and mixed forest passing the Tululusia waterfalls, just 15 minutes to the gate with possibility of seeing wildlife in the open glade. Arrive Momela gate.

Accommodation for you hike

Two person hut for hikers on mount Meru, Miriakamba hut around 2500metres and saddle hut around 3500 metres .
I public campsite.
2 special campsites in the Montana forest at the foot of mount Meru and the Ngurudoto crater .
Other accommodation is available outside the park in usa river town and variety option in Arusha town.
No lodges inside the park, but the Momella lodge and the Hatari lodge are on its boundary.

Swahili phrases

-Welcome –Karibu
-Thanks – Asante
-Thanks very much- Asante sana
-No – Hapana
-Yes – Ndiyo
-No thank you – Hapana asante
-Yes please – Ndiyo tafadhali
-What's up – Mambo
-Cool – Poa
-Hello – Jambo
-Grate – Babukubwa
-Congratulation – Hongera
- slowly- Polepole
- Sorry – Pole
-Please – Tafadhali
-Cold – Baridi
-Worm – Joto
- Hot water – Maji moto
-Tea - Chai
- Water – Maji
-Snow – Barafu
-Banana – Ndizi
-Mango – Maembe
-Avocado –Parachichi
-Orange – Chungwa
-Lion – Simba
- Elephant – Tembo
-Leopard –Chui
-Buffalo – Mbogo
-Rhino- Faru
-Cheetah – Duma
-Giraffe- Twiga
-Good bye - Kwaheri

**Thank you!!!
Can I ask
a favor?**

We see you've made it all the way to the end of our book. We're so glad you enjoyed it enough to get all the way through! If you liked it, would you be kind enough to leaving us a 4 or 5 star review please? You see, we're self published authors, and when people like you are able to give us positive reviews, it helps us out in a big way.

It'd really mean a lot to us.

Thank you!

Ari/Wayne (Joe)

About the Authors

As a Chief Guide on Kilimanjaro, Aristarick Benard has been conquering Kilimanjaro for the past 6 years. He was born on the base of the mountain, learnt his trade carrying kit bags and then qualified as a professional tour guide from a College in Arusha. He has helped many climbers get to the top and works with local Tour companies. Currently a twiga explorer, having been to the roof of Africa more than 80 times.

Wayne (Joe) Evans, lives in Cardiff, in the UK and has three beautiful daughters who are his total inspiration! He spends his free time (surprisingly) walking (hopefully up mountains), but runs various companies since 1998.

Llwyddiant! (Success to you!)

Ari & Joe.

If you'd like more information about me and would like to stay in touch, please come to my blog, at http://www.joefizz.com

Other books available from me at:
https://www.amazon.com/author/wayneevans

Made in the USA
San Bernardino, CA
25 February 2017